THE WONDER OF CHILDHOOD

THE WONDER OF CHILDHOOD

René Querido

RSCP

The following are revised and edited transcripts of lectures delivered by René Querido. Reprinting is made possible by a grant from The Waldorf Curriculum Fund

Cover: painting by Beppe Assenza entitled *Schritt ins Leben* (Stepping into Life), © Gideon Spicker Verlag, Uraweg 14, 4143 Dornach, Switzerland..

Reprinted 2002

ISBN 0-945803-08-7

Book orders may be made through
Rudolf Steiner College Bookstore
Tel. 916-961-8729, FAX 916-961-3032
E-mail: bookstore@steinercollege.edu

Rudolf Steiner College Press
9200 Fair Oaks Boulevard
Fair Oaks, CA 95628, U.S.A.

THE MIRACLE

OF

CHILDHOOD

THE MIRACLE OF CHILDHOOD

A great deal of interest has been stirred since the 1960's investigations relating to life-after-life. The work of Raymond Moody and Elisabeth Kübler-Ross has offered not only comfort but a new understanding to many. If we can gain certainty as to the reality of life after death, another question no less compelling arises: does the soul exist before birth—or do we arise only through the biological act of procreation? Recently, as though to proclaim that we *are* more than a biochemical result, much care has been lavished practically and emotionally on the entry of the baby out of the womb into life: this passage should be made as harmonious and untraumatic as possible. Birth is a beautiful experience.

Thomas Traherne (1637-1674), a little-known British Romantic poet whose name is frequently linked with such nineteenth century poets as Blake and Wordsworth, was able to capture the mood of the soul entering upon its earthly pilgrimage:

How like an angel came I down!
How bright are all things here!
When first among his works I did appear,
O how their glory did me crown!
The World resembled His eternity,
In which my soul did walk;
And everything that I did see
Did with me talk.

In seven further verses of the poem entitled "Wonder," Thomas Traherne describes with infinite delicacy how everything appears irradiated with light to the newborn child immediately after his or her arrival from a heavenly world. The poet speaks of a Paradise consciousness that surrounds the child with divine innocence and hides what is ugly, evil and perverse from him. "When I was born," he says, "everything that I did see did with me talk"—a perfect union with nature and all its creatures prevailed.

Wordsworth (1770-1850), one of the greatest Romantic poets, lived close to nature and was endowed with an almost uncanny faculty for remembering his early childhood. He was also able to express his intimations of events that occurred in the realm of the soul before birth in the ode "From Recollections of Early Childhood":

Our birth is but a sleep and a forgetting;
The soul that rises with us, our life's star,
Hath had elsewhere its setting,
And cometh from afar:
Not in entire forgetfulness
And not in utter nakedness,
But trailing clouds of glory do we come
From God, who is our home:
Heaven lies about us in our infancy!

Wordsworth continues and paints the picture of how the "shades of the prison-house begin to close upon the growing boy." The celestial light fades for the youth and "the man perceives it die away and fade into the light of common day." That is why we feel every birth is a miracle—an event full of wonder—because a being of divine origin has come to earth.

In both these poems—and many others express similar sentiments—the soul is seen as existing before birth; the gradual process of incarnation (literally "entering into the flesh") is experienced as a loss of divine participation which is gradually replaced by an adaptation to earthly tasks through the awakening of the capacities of thinking, feeling and willing—through the development of mind, heart and strength for deed.

Let us now attempt to examine more closely the process of the development during the first three years—marked by three "miracles." The work of Rudolf Steiner (1861-1925) has inspired us deeply. He is the inaugurator of the Waldorf school movement (nursery/kindergarten through high school) now represented worldwide by approximately 500 schools. (Over 100 Waldorf schools exist on the North American continent—United States, Canada and Mexico.) Steiner has provided us with some of the clearest descriptions of the child's "coming down" (i.e., stages of development) that are available, and it is out of an appreciation and understanding of these pictures of child development that our own following considerations have evolved.

No sensitive mother—or father, for that matter—can but be impressed by the remarkable change that especially a first-born brings into their lives. The advent of a child is far more than the result of a mere biological set of facts that have been accurately investigated in the past one hundred years. A sense of wonder arises as we observe lovingly how the helpless baby, instinctively demanding so much for its own needs, gradually manifests its own individuality, and, in the course of time, becomes a responsible, upright, conscious human being.

The first stage, from being carried to crawling on all fours, to standing and walking upright, is an immense achievement. No animal, however highly developed, can free its extremities from the pull of the earth so as to work. But consider the human hand with its incomparable, varied possibilities. Consider the hands of the carpenter, the hands and agile fingers of the seamstress, of the pianist, of the surgeon—hands that are engaged in incredibly subtle, complicated activity, or that serve other human beings, or hands joined in prayer.

Only the human being can grow into moral and inner uprightness. All this is connected with the development of the first year. The emerging individuality of the child finds its way, its path in life through the act of walking upright. It foreshadows what later can be understood at a deeper level as "I am the Way," according to the Gospel of St. John.

In the second year, the childlike babbling of unintelligible sounds which delight us turns into comprehensible language. We learn our native mother tongue (there do not appear to be "father" tongues—eine Muttersprache, une langue maternelle, etc.) through imitation—and indeed the mother here, as also in feeding, plays a central part. Mother's words of endearment, when spoken or sung, feed the soul of her baby. It has been well established that words nourish and the lack of speech seriously deprives the growing child.

In fact, we are capable of learning some 1200 languages (plus the many thousands of dialects) if only we are exposed to them early enough. The wish to communicate through speech comes naturally through imitation. If there were no one to speak to us we would not learn to do so. But again, this form of communication, intimately connected with the beat of heart and lung—with the middle portion of our physical structure, between head and limb—has many levels. We learn to speak before we consciously think. Rudolf Steiner in his many lectures stresses as early as 1919 that speech is born out of movement, and that thinking awakens out of speech. These three activities—movement, speech, thought—arise out of the development of the first three years of the life of the child.

Animals make sounds, birds sing and thus communicate, but only at an instinctive level. They cannot achieve what the human being can: to express creatively by way of language what lives within the heart and mind (through poetry, in prose, in dialogue). The human word enables us to communicate the essence of what lives within us to another individual. Over the years languages themselves (both the spoken and the written word) evolve and are altered by those who use them. It is remarkable, for instance, how radically English, French, German and Spanish have changed over the last hundred years. We do not only communicate, we also commune with one another through language. Through the word we become social human beings. We exchange what lives within us, our joys or fears, our aspirations and our hopes for the future. In the use of the word, we are constantly struggling towards the truth that can unite us. We know that lies, deception, untruths destroy the social fabric that is woven between one human being and another. The basis for trust and confidence lies, not only in deeds but also in how we speak to one another. Quite rightly, a sense of integrity is still attached to the saying "I give you my word." In learning to speak in the early years of childhood, we aspire toward what we find expressed in the Gospel of St. John as "I am the Truth."

In the third year of the child's life, a third miracle is accomplished. Whereas walking is essentially connected with the limb-metabolic pole of being, placed in the lower part of the body, and the second phase of speaking is centered in the rhythmic system, in the heart and lung area, the third stage of development encompasses the head organization, the nerve-and-sense system. The child in this third year develops three essential faculties that will shape the rest of his or her life.

I was present once when a little boy of about three said to his mother triumphantly, "Mummy, I am I and you are you!" This is more far-reaching than just one of those things that children say. When the child utters "I" for the first time we witness the awakening of his or her own individuality, of that unique self that makes him or her different from anyone else.

Without becoming too philosophical, it is a fact that no one can say "I" to another. However much we may be connect with someone else, however much we may love him or her, that other one is always a "you"—"you and I" are "we." We can only say "I" to ourselves, each for himself, for herself. This signals the separation of "self" and "world"—here am "I" and there, separate from myself are "you." Through love a bridge can be built that unites "you" and "I"—that is the meaning of relationships at many different levels—but the sense of individual identity will always remain, even in the act of becoming "we."

With this consciousness of self, of the "I am," the activity of thinking dawns—an inner process from this moment onward begins to awaken a faculty that is essentially human. No animal can say or experience "I" and "world"—or think about what lives around it or takes place within its inmost being. Only the human being can achieve this—and this second faculty remains a growing capacity throughout the whole of life.

This is accompanied by a third component. As we look back on life and try to fathom our first memory, we find that we have to rely on parents and relatives to help place that first recollection in time and often also in space. There are, of course, telling exceptions, such as the poems quoted above by William Wordsworth and Thomas Traherne. This interesting experiment of looking back to find our first memory which everyone should undertake, reveals that, in general, we began to remember around the age of three. Most people cannot recall what happened in their own childhood before that threshold. Our crawling, our walking, our first attempts at words are usually shrouded in mystery. Memory begins when we learn from within to say "I" and when thinking arises as a newly acquired faculty.

The importance of "thinking" in human activities cannot possibly be denied—it is the source of freedom, or individual responsibility. We become ourselves through the quality of our "thought"; it should neither be cold and abstract, nor vague and fuzzy. We strive for a thinking which is flexible, lively, creative. In the third year of the child's development, a third theme is sounded: "I am the Life," as found in the Gospel of St. John. Life-giving forces are awakened in the consciousness of self, in the inner activity of thought, in the power of memory.

We have attempted to show that in the first three years of a child's development "miracles" are accomplished before our very eyes that will determine the destiny of the individual for the rest of his or her life on earth. And now, little by little, the child will commence to shape and fashion his or her own biography—which literally means "life-writing." But of what does this life-writing, this biography that is unique to each one of us, consist? Of deeds (engaging our limbs), of feelings and emotions (born of the heart), of thoughts and aspirations (conceived in the head). The basis for this in all of us—in the greatest man or woman, in the humblest person—is laid down in the first three years of life.

Without a doubt, heredity and environment play important roles in the fashioning of our natures, in the forming of our character. Family life and education are powerful factors and should be reckoned with, but over and above this, infusing will, heart and mind with its specific genius, is the creative, unique Self, that "I" that in Wordsworth's words "cometh from afar." Such thoughts, once they begin to stir our hearts and minds, are of immense consequence. It means that the child brings something with him, with her—does not start from scratch with an unwritten page (the *tabula rasa* of the materialists of the last century), but is endowed from before birth with innate faculties beyond what is offered in the stream of heredity and environment.

The first three years may be compared to the overture of an opera where the main themes are sounded and are then, in the course of life, elaborated and transformed in accordance with our destinies. Is it not the task of parents and teachers alike to become more sensitive, more attentive to what the child strives to impart of its own essential being as it unfolds?

Education rightly understood seeks to "bring forth," and not merely to instruct, to "put in." Herodotus (c. 484-424 BC), the Greek historian, rightly said: "Education is not to fill a bucket, it is to kindle a fire." It is our hope that this article may throw a new light on the wonder of childhood and contribute in some measure to the rediscovery of human values in the upbringing and education of our children.

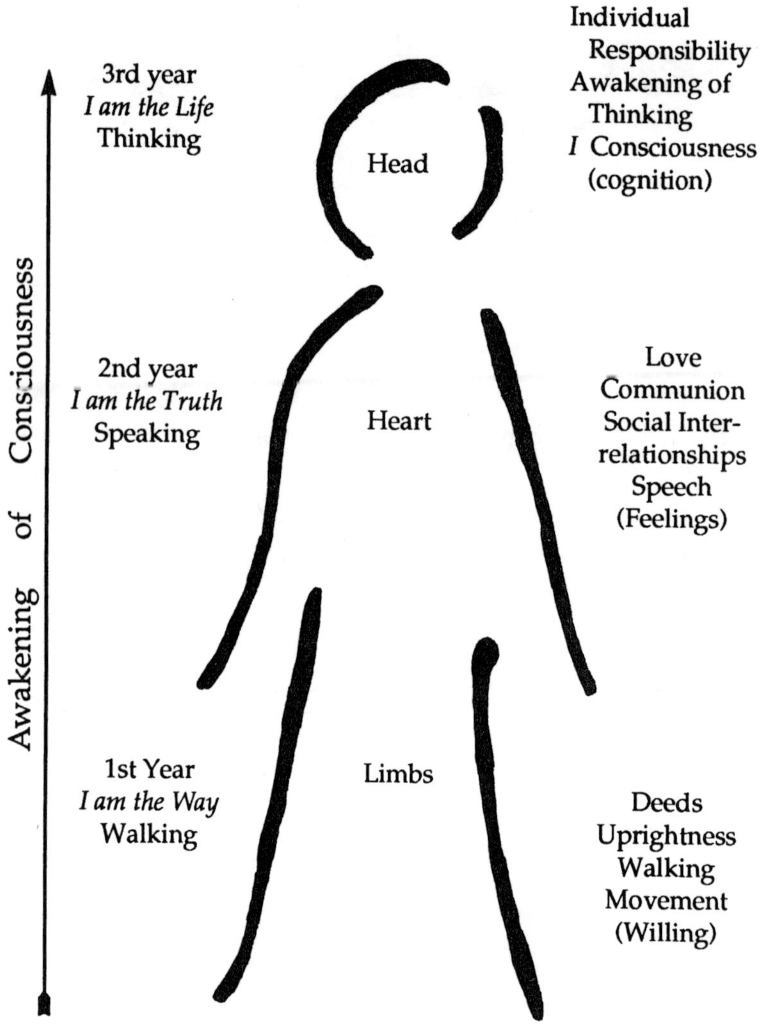

The First Three Years of the Child

from DUMNESS

by

Thomas Traherne

Sure Man was born to Meditat on Things
And to Contemplat the Eternal Springs
Of God and Nature, Glory, Bliss and Pleasure;
That life and Love might be his Heavenly Treasure:
And therefore Speechless made at first, that he
Might in himself profoundly busied be:
And not vent out, before he hath t'ane in
Those Antidots that guard his Soul from sin.

Wise Nature made him Deaf too, that he might
Not be disturbd, while he doth take Delight
In inward Things, nor be depravd with Tongues,
Nor Injurd by the Errors and the Wrongs
That Mortal Words Convey . . .

This, my Dear friends, this was my Blessed Case;
For nothing spoke to me but the fair Face
Of Heav'n and Earth, before my self could speak,
I then my bliss did, when my Silence, break.
My Non-Intelligence of Human Words
Ten thousand Pleasures unto me affords; . . .

Then did I dwell within a World of Light,
Distinct and Separat from all Mens Sight,
Where did I feel strange Thoughts, and such Things
see
That were, or seemed, only reveald to Me.
There I saw all the World Enjoyd by one;
There I was in the World alone;
No Business Serious seemd but one; No Work
But one was found; and that did in me lurk.

D'ye ask me What? It was with Cleerer Eys
To see all creatures full of Deities;
Especially Ones self: And to Admire
The Satisfaction of all True Desire
Twas to be Pleasd with all that God had done;
Twas to Enjoy even All beneath the sun:
Twas with a Steddy and immediat Sense
To feel and measure all the Excellence
Of Things: Twas to inherit Endless Treasure,
And to be filld with Everlasting Pleasure:
To reign in Silence and to Sing alone
To see, love, Covet, have, Enjoy and Prais, in one:
To prize and prais. Thus was I pent within
A Fort, Impregnable to any Sin:
Till the Avenues being Open laid,
Whole Legions Enterd, and the Forts Betrayed.

Before which time a Pulpit in my Mind,
A Temple, and a Teacher I did find,
With a large text to comment on. No Ear,
But Eys them selvs were all the Hearers there.
And evry Stone, and evry Star a Tongue,
And evry Gale of Wind a Curious song.
The Heavens were an Oracle, and spake
Divinity: the Earth did undertake
The office of a Priest; And I being Dum
(Nothing besides was dum;) All things did com
With Voices and Instructions; but when I
Had gained a Tongue, their Power began to die . . .

Yet the first Words mine Infancy did hear,
The Things which in my Dumness did appear,
Preventing all the rest, got such a root
Within my Heart, and stick so close unto't
It may be Trampled on, but still will glow;
And Nutriment to Soyl it self will owe.
The first Impressions are Immortal all.
And let Mine Enemies hoop, Cry, roar, or Call,
Yet these will whisper if I will but hear,
And penetrat the Heart, if not the Ear.

from MY SPIRIT

An Object, if it were before
Mine Ey, was by Dame Nature's Law
Within my Soul: Her Store
Was all at once within me; all her Treasures
Were my immediat and internal Pleasures;
Substantial Joys, which did inform my Mind.

. . . I could not tell
Whether the Things did there
Themselves appear,
Which in my Spirit truly seem'd to dwell;
Or whether my conforming Mind
Were not ev'n all that therein shin'd.

THE PREAPARATIVE

My Body being dead, my Limbs unknown;
        Before I skill'd to prize
        Those living Stars, mine Eys;
Before or Tongue or Cheeks I call'd mine own,
    Before I knew these Hands were mine,
Or that my Sinews did my Members join;
    When neither Nostril, Foot, nor ear,
As yet could be discern'd or did appear;
        I was within
A House I knew not; newly cloath'd with Skin.

Then was my soul my only All to me,
        A living endless Ey,
        Scarce bounded with the Sky,
Whose Power, and Act, and Essence was to see;
    I was an inward Sphere of Light,
Or an interminable Orb of Sight,
    Exceeding that which makes the Days,
A vital Sun that shed abroad its Rays:
        All Life, all Sense,
A naked, simple, pure Intelligence.

THOUGHTS

Ye brisk Divine and Living Things.
Ye great Exemplars, and ye Heavenly Springs,
Which I within me see;
Ye Machines Great,
Which in my Spirit God did Seat,
Ye Engines of Felicitie . . . .

RAPHAEL'S *SISTINE MADONNA*

Is It Appropriate for the Kindergarten?

RAPHAEL'S *SISTINE MADONNA*

Is It Appropriate in the Kindergarten?

Of the countless masterpieces of Renaissance painting, perhaps none occupies such a remarkable position as the *Sistine Madonna* by Raphael. It embodies in a superb manner great contrasts: the painting is both magnificent and intimate in character, heavenly and earthly in mood, sacred and secular in portraying the mysteries of motherhood and the eternal feminine.

Raphael (1483-1520), who was born on Good Friday and died on Good Friday at the early age of 37, is said to have painted the *Sistine Madonna* a few years before his death—at thirty-four or thirty-five. It therefore belongs to the artist's later period. Although it served as an altarpiece for a number of years, the original intention for it may have been a very different one. Executed on canvas rather than on a wooden panel as was the custom, it may have been painted expressly to be carried in processions through the crowded streets of Rome at high festivals of the Virgin Mary. This would also suggest that it was meant, in spite of its magnificence and considerable size, to be a work of art for the people at large and not simply for the clergy or nobility.

For the past 250 years or so it has had as its home the National Gallery in Dresden, until recently in East Germany, a once beautiful city struck by a most tragic destiny at the end of the Second World War, when thousands upon thousands of inhabitants were killed in a senseless bombing raid. The painting has survived this and the many other vicissitudes of wars, revolutions and insurrections from the 18th century onwards and has counted among its admirers such various and distinguished personalities as Goethe, Novalis and Dostoyevski.

Today one approaches the original canvas, measuring some eight or nine feet in height (for the figures are life size), from the end of a long gallery. The experience as one slowly moves toward the *Madonna* is indeed truly overwhelming, for as one draws near, one senses that the central figure carrying the child gently strides toward the beholder like some supersensible revelation. With the green curtains on either side drawn, we seem to cross a threshold into a heavenly realm where against a background of numberless angelic faces, and supported by billowing clouds, the mystery of motherhood and of Mary with the child is revealed. The central female figure combines a serene, divine countenance with great earthly beauty. Raphael may well have been inspired by one of his many beautiful models, but here he transformed the experience into a heavenly countenance. The child is remarkably awake and knowing for one so young, as if aware of the thorny road that he is destined to tread on the earth.

Too little attention has been given to the two saints that flank the central figure. They form an intrinsic part of the composition as indeed do the two winged cherubic beings at the foot of the painting who peek up at the events with a quiet, somewhat mischievous, childlike curiousity.

Saint Sixtus II, a magnificent old man clad in golden papal robes, is seen on our left looking up in deep reverence and conscious recognition at the mother and child. His right arm and hand point outwards to the beholder while his left hand rests with a warm, sympathetic gesture on his heart.

In strong contrast we have on our right a portrayal of the young, beautiful Saint Barbara whose head is turned with lowered gaze toward us, her hands folded in devotion across her breast.

The historical background of these two figures will give further meaning to the total composition. Both Saint Barbara (235-313) and Sixtus II (Pope: 257-258) lived in Italy during the third century AD when the original Christ impulse in its fullness had not yet been impeded by church dogma and state approval.

Barbara, renowned for her beauty, was locked up in a tower by her father who feared that she had become a Christian. She maintained her faith and suffered horrible torture which left her disfigured for life. Her father ordered her killed, but legend tells us that as the execution was to be accomplished he was struck by lightning. Saint Barbara lived into her late seventies and was known for her loving, caring deeds for the poor and ailing.

Sixtus II, who only occupied the papal chair for one year, was able at a time of terrible conflict to bring about peace. He did so by renouncing power. Widely admired for his magnanimity and benevolence, he was canonized shortly after his death and was regarded with special veneration, by many generations right up to the Renaissance.

These two biographical vignettes will help us to understand Raphael's wise choice in portraying just these particular saints on either side of Mary and the Child. They represent archetypes: Sixtus of power transformed into peace, Barbara of the sacrifice of beauty into spiritual love, both inspired by the eternal feminine, the bearer of the child. Indeed if then we view the central figure also as a divine archetype made manifest on earth in all her glory, beauty and inner serene strength, this masterpiece is lifted out of any one-sided, dogmatic interpretation. It is not merely a Christian painting in the narrow sense of the word. It can appeal strongly and intimately to men and women of any religious persuasion—Christians, Jews, Buddhists alike—if it is seen as representing an ideal of conscious yet eternal motherhood carrying the child as he awakens from innocence to strong deeds of love. Such representations are also found in other cultures: in Isis and the child Horus in Egypt, in the Kwan Yin or Kanon of the Orient.

Let us now deal with the question: should a reproduction of the Sistine Madonna necessarily be displayed in Waldorf kindergartens, and if so, why?

In Waldorf Education the importance of harmony and beauty in a child's surroundings has often been emphasized. Especially in the early stages of his or her development the child is a sensitive sense organ. Not only do children delight in what they receive through their senses, but wholesome, therapeutic or negative and undesirable influences can flow through what they see, hear and touch. If, for instance, we place in a child's bedroom, or in the kindergarten, a reproduction of the

Sistine Madonna by Raphael, whether we draw the child's attention to it or not, the presence of the picture alone will have a healing, calming effect on the child's soul.

For the genius of the artist was such that this painting so embodies the archtypal ideals of the eternal feminine, of power transformed into peace, and of the sacrifice of earthly beauty for spiritual love, as well as the experience of standing at the threshold of the realms of the Spirit, that the young child, who can carry no intellectual concepts of the content of this painting, nonetheless directly experiences and is nurtured by the truths which it so beautifully portrays. It is indeed difficult to imagine anything in the child's environment which could be more reassuring and nurturing to a being newly-arrived in our difficult world. Even if the child never gazes directly at the *Sistine Madonna,* its message of the existence of a divine, nurturing love flanked by loving personal transformation and sacrifice, with the spiritual realms standing, as it were, behind these ideals, will nevertheless penetrate and sustain his or her wondering soul.

Rudolf Steiner was aware of the effects of such works of art when, in 1911, he gave indications to Dr. Peipers in Munich that a healing influence proceeds from contemplating again and again a series of Madonnas in reproduction arranged in the form of a pentagram. The series of 15 pictures, mostly Madonnas by Raphael (there is one by Donatello and one by Michelangelo), opens with the *Sistine Madonna,* whose composition itself is clearly based on the pentagram, and culminates in Raphael's *Transfiguration,* his last, unfinished painting.

Astonishingly powerful healing can be obtained even when the pictures are reproduced in black and white, as was the case in Steiner's time when he gave the indications to Dr. Peipers for his patients. (Today the series is readily available in colored post cards.)

How are we to understand this process? We are familiar with the soul strengthening that can be received by meditating regularly on a verse or mantra. Such words—and Rudolf Steiner has provided us with hundreds of verses for particular occasions—contain through their content, sound, cadence and composition a seed power that awakens new faculties in the soul. For the teacher this is of special significance, for such inner activity regularly practiced in the stillness of the soul makes us more able to cope with our task of caring for and educating children.

What is perhaps less familiar is the use of the Yantra, as it is known in the East: a picture, a scroll of calligraphy (as particularly practiced by the Japanese), or a statue which, through its mere presence in a hall, a place of worship, or a private room, endows the space with an uplifting mood. Space, color and form can exert a direct, beneficent healing influence and are able to awaken, under certain circumstances, dormant spiritual powers in the beholder.

In the light of the above, we need to tread a balanced path between over-sentimentality and cold abstraction in determining the role of the *Sistine Madonna* in the kindergarten. To exclude this masterpiece altogether seems foolish. If objections to its presence arise on religious grounds, we should attempt to present a wider viewpoint. I am not suggesting that some of the above considerations should be voiced indiscriminately. What matters is that the teacher has come to an inner conviction over a period of time regarding the benefits of this painting and can speak to the hearts and minds of inquiring parents out of depth of personal experience.

It is equally inappropriate to build an altar draped with colored veils around the *Sistine Madonna.* A shrine-like display with candles will justifiably create uneasiness in many parents, even among those who are genuinely interested in the new mysteries revealed through Anthroposophy. Our task therefore is a difficult one: to learn to appreciate that this superb masterpiece combines a serene, sober mood with divine revelation and is utterly devoid of sentimentality. Can we therefore accord the *Sistine Madonna* a special place in the kindergarten room in a simple, straightforward manner, bearing in mind that the children's attention need not be drawn to it? It acts in a healing, peaceful manner through its very presence.

It may also be helpful to consider whether it would not be preferable to display the full reproduction in a large print (considering the size of the original) rather than making do with a portion of the painting. This is especially so because the flanking figures express through gesture and mood the qualities of peace and love. The cherubic figures at the foot of the painting contribute a delightful quality of childlike innocence.

This theme is of special importance in our time when we should penetrate what we do as educators with growing understanding.

Other books by René Querido
published by Rudolf Steiner College Press

Creativity in Education
The Esoteric Background of Waldorf Education
Geography and Man's Responsibility for the Earth
The Golden Age of Chartres
The Mystery of the Holy Grail
Questions and Answers on Reincarnation and Karma

Behold I Make All Things New (with Hilmar Moore)